GREAT
IDEAS FOR
VBS

By John R. Cutshall

Illustrated by Michael Streff

STANDARD
PUBLISHING
Cincinnati, Ohio

Help 390

Scripture quotation is from The Holy Bible, New International Version, ©1973, 1978, 1984, International Bible Society. Used by permission of Zondervan Bible Publishers.

Library of Congress Cataloging-in-Publication Data

Cutshall, John R. (John Robert), 1959-
    Great ideas for VBS / John R. Cutshall.
        p.   cm.
    Includes index.
    ISBN 0-87403-675-5
    1. Vacation schools, Christian. I. Title.   II. Title: Great ideas for
Vacation Bible School.
BV1585.C87 1992
268--dc20   91-28461
                                                                        CIP

Dedication

Dedicated to my dad, John Ray Cutshall, who taught me how to dream–my life has never been the same–and to my mom, Kaye Cutshall, whose words I remember to this day: "Get out from in front of that TV set and do something creative!" I guess she was right. Maybe I should have listened to her more often. With love, J.B.

CONTENTS

INTRODUCTION

On one of those rare days when nothing was pressing, I found myself heading downstairs to begin a day of doing "manly" things. The items on my agenda include eating, watching the ball game on TV, and a bit of casual reading.

As I reached the kitchen, I greeted my wife and she smiled. She asked about my night's sleep and wished me the best for the day—just as she handed me a list. "Today is 'Honey-do Day'!" she pleasantly informed me. "You get to help me out around the house. I've got a list of jobs and 'honey' you get to 'do' them." I fumbled with the list of jobs that she had handed me and I knew I was in trouble when I discovered it was written on an old roll of wall paper that measured twenty-five feet in length.

Once again, I found myself reaching for my trusty toolbox. I like my toolbox. Its four red walls house tools of every size, shape, and purpose. With these tools I can finish many projects and chores that otherwise would be impossible. I can hammer nails, tighten loose bicycle wheels, and, in a few hours, shrink a list of "do's" into a tally of "dones."

I have found that in building a better Vacation Bible School, I need some very special tools. Luckily, these handy-dandy little helpers are easy to find — if you know where to look. The chapters in this book hold ideas, or tools, that help in planning and presenting any VBS program. These ideas can function independently of one another or interdependently with each other. Don't feel that you need to incorporate every idea. Use it as a catalog from which you can pick and choose, not a recipe book in which you take each of the steps in order. Consider this book as your VBS toolbox.

Building a better Vacation Bible School is quite a "Honey-do" list. Whether you are a first year "rookie" or a seasoned "veteran" director, you will need quality tools, fine materials, and skilled workers. Much depends on the results of your labors. So reach for the toolbox and let's go!

1

PURPOSE

DESIGNING A BLUEPRINT

 **Know Why You Have
a Vacation Bible School**

You can sponsor a Vacation Bible School for many
reasons, some good . . . some not so good. You need
to know why you have a VBS. Will your VBS reach
out to your community (evangelize)? Will it offer
intensive training for your own church (educate)? Is it
tradition (a poor reason for anything)? Know the
reason for your Vacation Bible School and make
everything you do point to this purpose. Don't use an

activity—even a good one—if it doesn't support your main thrust.

 ## 2 Scrutinize Your Statistics

Keeping records of everything improves your VBS. Once you have compiled the statistics, compare these to your goals and ask "Why are or aren't we reaching our goals?" Just asking and answering these questions will allow you to improve your VBS.

For some ideas on which records and statistics should be kept, see Appendix A on page 84.

 ## 3 Use Goals to Motivate—Think Big!

Goals motivate people, so make good use of them. Whether attendance, offering, registrations, percent of congregation involved, or number of cookies served set goals for everything and communicate your goals to your church.

 ## 4 To Raise Your Goal— Threaten Your Minister

When a congregation loves their minister, they love to see him exposed to non-lethal threats. Examples include a pie in the face, a dunk in the pool, a water balloon bombing, a long hike from point "A" to point "B," or a wheelbarrow ride through town. All would

work nicely. Remember, don't hurt the minister! Just put him in a fun situation. If he has a sense of humor, it should be no problem at all. It always works best if you ask his permission before you announce it to your congregation.

 Think Like a Teacher

In preparing for VBS, stop a minute to think like a teacher. Ask questions like "What do our activities teach?," "What can I do to allow the gospel to better affect the lives of my students?," and "What else can we do, inside and outside of the classroom, to teach?" If you think like a teacher, good answers will emerge for these questions.

 ## 6   Think Like a Child

The second of the three "thinks" is to think like a child. Put yourself in a child's frame of mind. Does your VBS sound and look like fun? Would you, as a child, want to come back? By thinking at different age perspectives, you improve the quality of your VBS. Its impact upon the lives of your students will dramatically increase.

 ## 7   Think Like a Parent

Equally important in our think list is to think like a parent. You will gain parents' favor through proper preparation. Walk through your entire VBS from a parent's perspective. Does it show that you care for "my" child? Do you see quality? Do you see love? Do you notice good organization? Asking these questions from a parents perspective can and will make a difference.

2

PLANNING

POURING THE CONCRETE

8 Don't Be Afraid to Dream

Just because you've never done VBS that way before, doesn't mean you can't do something bigger, better, or different. Before the Wright brothers no one had ever flown. Brainstorm possibilities. Don't throw out any idea, no matter how wild. Take a look at your reasons for having a VBS, then shoot for the stars. You can always accomplish more, but only if you dream it first.

9 Use a Directing Committee

Millions of details cover Vacation Bible School. It would overwhelm just one person. Use a committee where each person has a specific area to supervise. A committee divides recruiting into friend circles. It spreads out the responsibility and allows others to share in the success of VBS. You could be a chairperson, but you won't like a solo act.

For an example of organizing your VBS with a directing committee see the diagram in Appendix B on page 86.

 ## 10 Pay Attention to Details

Remember, in a successful VBS there are the over-all plans, but it's the details that people will notice. Do you start on time? Is the church building clean? Do you have enough scissors? Do your people smile in the hallways at the visitors when they pass? The only way to take care of the little details is to make a list before VBS begins and then check it out just before each night's program. You see, the little things aren't so little.

 ## 11 Write Job Descriptions

When things go wrong and Murphy's Law again proves itself true, do you ever find yourself thinking,

"Don't they know they were suppose to be responsible for that?" Maybe they don't. Plan to avoid problems and miscommunications by writing job descriptions. Be specific in the objectives of each job. Explain in detail each responsibility, and be helpful with your hints. Your volunteers will be better informed and it will also help you clarify what you are asking them to do.

For examples of VBS job descriptions, see Appendix C on page 87.

 Personal Attention Is the Key to Success

"People win people, programs don't." This old adage still rings true. The more personal attention you plan into your VBS, the more successful it will be. Personal attention may mean more workers, smaller classes or both. It may mean a more personal mind set and less of a "herd mentality," — you know, "It's time to herd them here; it's time to herd them there." Personal attention brings retention. Maybe we can start a new adage of our own.

 Pray

Many people acknowledge that prayer is important; however, their attitudes reflect, "OK, let's pray and then we'll get down to the real business at hand."

Prayer is the real business at hand! Success depends upon involving the Lord from beginning to closing.

 **Prayer Warriors Idea #1:
Use Your Senior Saints**

"VBS is for the young people." That myth prevails among our "senior" saints. How far from the truth! Your senior saints can provide a great source of prayer support. Give them prayer lists, prayer reminders, "I'm proud to be a prayer warrior" buttons or anything that will involve them in VBS.

 **Prayer Warriors Idea #2:
Assign People to Pray for People**

People praying for people. Somehow it sounds so Biblical. "Carry each other's burdens, and in this way you will fulfill the law of Christ" (Galatians 6:2, *NIV*). After all your workers place their names in a bowl, have them draw out a different name. Each VBS volunteer will pray for the person whose name they drew. These secret prayer partners will add spiritual support to your VBS.

For a sample prayer list, see Appendix D on page 88.

 **Train Your Teachers
With a Minimum of Three Meetings**

VBS centers around your teachers. Train them! Bring any item, no matter how small, to their attention.

Hold at least three sessions for teacher training. You should catch your absentees from one meeting to another, so that they can be informed. These meetings should cover every detail. Training should start at least two months in advance of your VBS date. The enthusiasm will spread, and your VBS will show excitement and quality from the core out

 ## 17 Attempt to Keep VBS Rooms and Sunday School Rooms the Same

Keep your VBS rooms the same as your Sunday School rooms. This will cut down on confusion when a visitor returns to your church. The student will feel comfortable with their surroundings and will feel more at home.

 ## 18 Change the Time of Day

Why do you have VBS in the morning? Why do you have it in the evening? If you are not absolutely sure, try an experiment. Change the time of day VBS is usually held at your church. Go to evenings, if you're used to mornings or vice versa. The change of time would wake up some people to the idea that this VBS will be different.

 ## 19 Change Your Location

Changing the location of VBS may make a big impact on your attendance. Moving VBS to a farm or a park, for example, may change the personality of your VBS. It sounds like a simple idea, but it is effective.

 20 Day Camp

Meet at the designated spot and take VBS on the road. A day camp VBS is a great way to reach those who feel uncomfortable in churches. Develop a schedule that allows for both travel time and your regular program. According to the length of your schedule you may be able to include hikes, special classes, swimming, or other special events. At closing time, return to the drop-off station and prepare to do it again the next day. Day camp can be a great way to develop relationships with others in your community.

 21 Add a VBS Field Trip

Who says VBS has to be at the church every day of the week? Load up the entire crew and head out on a field trip to a farm or a museum. Have your lesson there. Drive to a prepared "Jerusalem" or "Calvary" to dramatize the lesson. VBS can be exciting no matter where it is, and a trip makes it even more special.

 22 Change the Time of Year

VBS doesn't have to be in the summer. Other vacations exist around the school year besides summer break. Move the traditional week of VBS to a new time of year. Publishers design VBS for any season and by changing the time of year, you've transmitted the message: "There is something special about this VBS!" Who knows — Spring break may never be the same!

 ## 23 Make VBS a Family Affair

VBS is for kids of all ages. It's true! Go beyond the grade school age level. Prepare classes and events for the entire family. Not only will the success of your labors increase, but it will help introduce entire families to each other, the church, and the Lord.

 ## 24 Develop a Patrol

You have things to move? Tables, chairs, crowds? Then form a patrol. A patrol is a group of people whose sole purpose is to help. They are on call to patrol traffic in the parking lot before and after VBS, move large furniture or props, and greet visitors. Your patrolman can be your best friend.

 ## 25 Form a "VBS Central" for Information and Phone Calls

As director or chairperson of the directing committee, how many times have you rushed to help someone and you are asked, "Did so-and-so find you?"

Designate an area as "VBS Central." You can post a "host" or "hostess" to give out information, receive phone calls, and take messages for you. As you touch base with "central" you will find VBS less confusing as information spreads more easily.

 26 **Develop an Evaluation Form and Use It**

To find out if the program met needs, you must ask the people. Do that through an evaluation. Keep it short and simple. Ask specific questions that require short answers. Then, hand them out to teachers. Expect only fifty percent or less of the evaluation forms to be returned. Tell the teachers that the forms are due the same day that they are handed out. The urgency of time will increase the return rate. You may find it difficult to take criticism, but the evaluation will help you develop a future VBS that meets the needs of the people.

See Appendix E on page 89 for a sample evaluation form.

3

RECRUITING

HIRING THE WORKERS

 27 **Recruiting Starts
at the Drawing Board**

Before you approach the first potential VBS worker, make sure you've got your blueprint in order. Figure out the number of workers needed. You can't expect people to agree to do "something in our VBS" and not know what that something is.

 28 **Pick the People Best for the Job**

When planning VBS, don't just fit names into each responsibility slot. Stop, pray, and consider who would be the best person for this job. Once you have identified the appropriate workers, recruit them. It sounds simple, but in the rush to get things done, this simple rule is often overlooked.

29 Involve the Men of Your Church

A dangerous myth is afoot: "VBS is women's work." Actually, students need both men and women as role models. VBS should reflect Christian relationships between the genders as examples to your students.

Arrange to have men become part of your VBS. You will find that men can be helpful.

30 Prayer Is Your Best Recruiting Tool

Once you've begun to think about recruiting, stop! Asking for help starts with God. He knows what jobs need to be done and who can do them best. Look over your list as you pray and when names come to mind, pencil them into the margins. Don't be surprised if you find yourself thinking of people that you wouldn't under normal circumstances. God has a way of expanding the limits of VBS beyond our circle of friends. Remember, make God your first recruit.

31 Let Others Do Your Recruiting for You

When you are looking for people to fill the positions of your Vacation Bible School staff, delegate a section to someone else. Allow teachers to recruit assistant teachers and craft workers. Let the recreation director find the right people to put his team over the top. Recruiting can be fun when you get to watch other people do the work.

32 Ask Your Minister

When it comes to knowing people, your minister is the person to ask. He may not have all the answers or all the people you need, but when it comes to personalities and talents, he's a resource that you can't afford to overlook.

33 If You See People Standing Still, Find Them a Job!

Vacation Bible School is an activity in which everyone can get involved. When you see someone standing around with nothing to do, make up a job. Not an insignificant chore but a responsibility that makes a difference. How about a front-door greeter or a table mover? How about placing VBS stickers on everyone who comes into the auditorium? A teacher-hugger is one of my favorites. Teachers need hugs.

34 Start at the End

Start recruiting at the end of your VBS. If a worker has done a good job, get them to start thinking about next year. This is not the time for the hard sell, but don't let this opportunity slip through your fingers. If VBS has gone well, then the people will be excited about what VBS can do. The "things that we can do to make next year's program better" are still fresh in their minds. If you start now your recruiting will be smoother next spring.

35 When Looking for Help, Use God's Eyes

VBS is a time for possibility and potential, not a time for fostering any kind of negativism. Don't allow personal differences to stand in the way of an opportunity. Another person may not do the job exactly the way that you would do it, but if their eyes are on God, then that's OK. If you look at a person's heart with the eyes of God, then a whole bunch of things don't seem as significant as they did before. Remember, if you look at people through the eyes of God, you're going need sunglasses because the recruiting prospects are going to be bright.

 Provide Child Care for Your Workers

When you go out looking to fulfill the needs of your VBS, don't forget the needs of your workers. Some mothers have babies and toddlers, but still want to volunteer for VBS. Provide a nursery. This will increase your work force and show the workers that you are thinking of their needs.

 When You Recruit, Think Negative

Someone in football once said "A good defense is the best offense." It works that way in recruiting too. Think negative for a moment, "Why would anyone say 'no' to an opportunity to work in VBS?" After you've made your list of reasons why people couldn't work, then start thinking of ways to help change *no's* to *yes's*.

4

PUBLICITY

BLASTING THE GOOD NEWS EVERYWHERE

38 Dust Off the Dynamite

When there is blasting on a building site, everyone knows about it. Somehow it's not one of those things that you can keep quiet. Everyone for miles around has heard the noise and wants to know what is happening. That's what you need to do with your publicity. Make enough noise to let people everywhere know what is happening. This is not the time or the place to be conservative. Be bold, be colorful, be loud! People

cannot and will not attend your program if they are not informed. So, dust off the dynamite and strike a match. It's time to make some noise!

 VBS Picture Flower Garden

Have each child's picture taken when they register. Use a polaroid and mark their names and address on the back. Another option is to use a 35mm camera one-hour film developing. Write a list of names in the order you took the pictures. You can also use large name tags on the children to help match the developed pictures and the vital information on your list. After you have the pictures in hand, post them on the wall as a part of a flower garden mural. This will excite parents and youth to see so many pictures. Also, after your VBS is over, it will help with name and face recall when you follow up on the students.

Move Your Stage Outdoors —Use a Hay Wagon

Move to the great outdoors! Your opening, closing, or even your entire VBS could be held outside. A hay wagon makes a great stage. Roll it into place, decorate it, and you've got a professional performing platform. You could even use a curtain or plywood sheets for a backdrop. You'll find that a hay wagon never looked so good! The possibilities for your VBS are as big as the great outdoors.

Have a VBS Pep Rally

Remember the feeling you had after your high school pep rally? You know, the one just before the big game? Why not throw a pep rally for VBS? Try skits, songs, cheers, and even a bonfire. You already have a rival team–Satan and his angels. A pep rally would be just the thing to create the excitement you need to get everyone pumped up for VBS.

Make Registration a Big Event

The VBS staff should encourage registration. Those names and addresses will help in following up prospective members after VBS is over. Make registration a big event. Give away a button, a balloon, a sticker, or a piece of candy to everyone who registers. Make an "I've Registered" honor roll and show off the names of those who have registered. The more importance you place on registration, the more complete your registration will become. Records are important.

 Make Your Registration Table Stand Out

Many of us use a registration table in the front lobby, but how many times does your table seem to blend into the scenery? Go the extra mile. Add color, sound, a slide display, balloons, blow-up figure, clowns, puppets, candy, animals, or anything else, to make your booth stand out! Enrollment and excitement will increase.

 Use "Storm Troopers" to Help Promote Registration

On a map, divide the area around the church into sections. Divide volunteers into groups, arm them with brochures advertising VBS, and let them go. Your "Storm Troopers" will spread the good news that your VBS is coming. Greet them with refreshments when they come back.

Use Bulletin Boards to Get the Word Out

Bulletin boards get the word out. Make them bold, bright, and three dimensional. Decorate them so that they will get the attention of anyone passing within three miles and you've got a winner. Take the extra time to do them right. People will judge the quality of your VBS by the quality of your bulletin board.

Newspaper Advertisement Idea #1: Ads

Paid advertisement in your local newspaper gets your message out to the people. It doesn't even have to be one of the bigger papers to be effective. Be original in your efforts. People will only look at what grabs their attention. Whether you use photographs, artwork, or creative wording, just get your VBS into print.

For samples of newspaper advertisements see Appendix F on page 91.

Newspaper Advertisement Idea #2 : Write a Story About Your VBS

OK, you can't afford an ad in the paper. No problem. Write a story about your VBS and send it into the paper. Find an angle to your VBS that is newsworthy and interesting to people who wouldn't otherwise care. Big numbers, offering totals, a story about your missionary, or maybe one of your special attention-getters could get you better coverage than money could buy!

48 Newspaper Advertisement Idea #3: Pictures Add Flair

Have a designated VBS photographer. Make sure he or she takes black and white pictures and sends the photos to the local paper. Free lance photography is accepted. If it's an extra special photo, it could clarify your image.

49 Advertise to a Specific Group of People

When you advertise your VBS, decide who you want to reach and with what specific advertisement method. Professionals call this developing a target audience. Stop and imagine your target audience and gear your method of advertisement to match their likes. A newspaper ad is good for adults and maybe teens (those who read the paper), but will not work for pre-school or grade schoolers. Handing out flyers to excite teens may be a great idea to try at the malls. Target your audience and your advertisement will become much more effective.

50 Bulletin Covers Really Get the Message Out!

Let your bulletin get the message out! Yes, announcements on the inside are important, but put your message on the outside cover too. Enlarge your VBS logo and reproduce it on bright colored paper. If you don't have a copier, then have the printing done at a quick print shop. Even if you don't use bulletins, this is a great attention-getter.

 ## Video Idea #1: Put Your VBS on TV

Use a video camera! Designate someone to be a camera person throughout the entire VBS. This is a great way to spread the news. Admit it. Everyone likes to see themselves on TV. You could even do a promotional commercial to play while you register people. Just point the camcorder and have the people wave to their friends at home!

 ## Video Idea #2: Use Last Year's Video to Promote VBS Registration

What do you do with your video after VBS is through? Save it and use it as promotion for next year's registration. Just run it next to your registration table and you'll draw a super-sized crowd.

 ## Use Table Cloth Paper and Make a VBS Mural

A roll of paper table covering stretches forever. Take one and line your hallways with it. A little adhesive tape or a few pins will hold it snugly in place. Then distribute crayons and allow the kids to draw things related to VBS. The children will take pride in their work. They'll bring family and friends to see it. It's great publicity and an inexpensive decoration.

Let Skits Promote for You

Shake your congregation out of the "announcement numbness" they've developed. Instead of simply having the minister announce VBS, perform a skit. A skit allows people to remember that your VBS is going to be quality. As always it should be short and rehearsed. A polished, well-presented skit will allow humor and information to flow, as well as create a great amount of anticipation. What a great way to use the creative talents of people in your congregation!

 Hang a Big Banner

It's not a new idea, but it's still a good one. Have a professional paint one for outside or have the kids create one of their own. Either way, big banners and lots of them will get your message through to the church and your community.

 Publish a Daily Newspaper

Publicize VBS in the homes of your students. Develop a daily newspaper. It could have statistics, daily events, and interviews from your director, minister, and missionary. Preview your summer or fall youth programming, Sunday school, or an upcoming event. Print it on bright paper and hand it out at the end of each day of VBS. Getting this information into the homes each night is invaluable.

The U.S. Mail
Delivers the Publicity You Want

Remember, as a child, receiving something in the mail? You taped it to the refrigerator door, you read it and reread it, and only after three weeks did you let your mother take it off the refrigerator door. VBS publicity can be the same way. Make it look good and put it in the mail. Check postage rates for bulk mailings and save money.

 ## Coloring Contests
Are Colorful Events

Get everyone involved in publicity for VBS. Have a coloring contest. Draw or copy a picture that promotes your VBS. Add the dates and a catchy phrase for your program. Then duplicate enough for everybody. After everyone has colored their picture have them sign their names on the front and hang them as posters around the church. The publicity is nearly free and it's a whole lot of fun.

 ## Strive to Be Unique

Will other churches be advertising the same VBS theme? Strive to be unique. Find something, or someone, about your church or VBS program that is special. It doesn't have to be extravagant, just different. Be creative.

5

PROGRAM

HITTING THE NAIL
ON THE HEAD

60 Hammer Time

Funny thing about a hammer. It's a good tool, but you always seem to end up using it on your thumb. Just for the record, that is not the best way to use a hammer. When this tool is used properly they call it "hitting the nail on the head." It works that way in programming also. When you've planned all the little details in advance, your VBS will hold together. If you've "missed," the pain can be excruciating. Start your programming early and make sure your swing is true. Then your VBS plans will be solid.

61 Terrific Thursdays — All Summer Long

Have you ever noticed that there are ten-day VBS kits and approximately the same number of weeks in the summer? Take advantage of the coincidence and have your regular VBS-type program one day a week for the entire ten weeks! It will be a great way to spread out the excitement and allow everyone to participate. It's great because no matter when your youth go to camp or on vacation, VBS will be there waiting for them when they return. It's a whole summer of VBS fun!

62 Program Like a Television Show

When watching TV, if there is any break in the regular flow of programming, you know somebody is not doing their job. You get impatient. You fidget. You get bored. The same can be true in your VBS. A break in the regular flow of the program can hurt your VBS enthusiasm. Plan so that everything will run logically, uniformly, and smoothly. Avoid "dead air time." This is time when nothing is happening and the students are left to their own resources for entertainment. You, as host, need to plan events on stage and in the classroom. This is a TV generation and they expect a well-rehearsed VBS.

63 Use Theater-Style Taped Music, Before and After VBS

Music plays everywhere you go. We just don't always notice it. It plays in the theaters, the restaurants, and the grocery stores. Establishments like these use music to calm their patrons and set an atmosphere. Use this principle to your advantage in VBS. Use "happy" music tapes before your opening, and use "excitement" music after your closing. It will add atmosphere and a professional feel to your total program.

64 There's Just Something About That Name

There is something special about a person's name. It is almost magical how it can break down barriers and warm up the atmosphere in a classroom. Name tags allow teachers to learn names and get closer to their students. You don't have to use the expensive ones; just use file folder labels or construction paper cut-outs and tape. A name tag can mean the difference between "Hey you!" and a personal touch of concern.

65 Making Your Opening Night Count

Your opening night should make the people want to attend VBS. Plan and polish the program until it transmits the message you desire. VBS deserves an opening equal to the unveiling of a new statue. Let your mind go and dream of all the possibilities. Most of all, shoot for an exciting, quality program that says "C'mon, it's a great week and we care enough to give you the very best!"

 ## Set Your Stage

Every show has a stage and every game show has a set. Don't sell yourself short. Set Your Stage! Dress it up to go along with your theme. Clear it of unnecessary clutter. Add some color and some lights.

The stage will look great, and will impress people with its professional appearance.

 ## Live Music

Are there musically-talented people in your congregation? If so, you have a gold mine of possibilities! Create a band to accompany your song service. Whether it's country, rock, rhythm and blues, or a kazoo/kitchen band, the live music adds fun and excitement. Live music gets attention and pleases the crowd.

 ## Taped Sing-Alongs

Is live music a problem? Don't feel bad. Find someone who can play the desired instrument(s) and prerecord your accompaniment. If your tape deck is appropriately loud, you will have scored points with the music you can provide.

 ## Make Your Missionary a Laboratory Experience

Missions are important! The VBS students need to understand missions, but how can someone accomplish something this important in the five to ten minutes of the opening or the closing? Have your missionary set up a specific area and allow each class to come in for a hands on, up close and personal look at your missionary. You can use this as a substitute for craft time one day. When the VBS students get to know the missionary personally it could be a life-changing event for them.

70   Use a Special Speaker

Your adults have been lured into a slumber by the myth that VBS is just for the kids. Wake them up! Use a special speaker for the adult class. Your class will be recognized as a special event and your adults will love it.

71   Make the Bible Come Alive

OK, so everybody else in town has the same VBS program as you. Be different! Dramatize the Bible stories. Go for the best you can do. Write the script. Most of them are vividly outlined in the Bible. Rehearse the players and present it live. Live dramatizations of Bible stories will make an impact on the VBS students.

72   Make the Bible Come Alive: The Sequel

Bible dramas are great, but just to be different, put them into a modern time frame. Take a Biblical story and modernize it. The Good Samaritan could become the Good Motorcycle Gang Member. The Prodigal Son could go to Las Vegas. The possibilities are endless.

73 Use Puppets

Everyone loves puppets. Use them in your opening, closing, classroom time, song service, or as an attention-getter. It takes some rehearsal, and timing is crucial, but the results are terrific.

74 Decorate

Decorate according to your theme. Decorate your stage, hallways, classrooms, bathrooms, entrances, front yard, backyard—you get the idea? Find a person who has a creative flair and let them go. The results will not only look good and build excitement, but the theme will be made clearer to the student.

75 Class Up Your Room!

Your classrooms are your learning laboratories. Make sure everything in you room points to your teaching goals. Decoration, posters, and banners help in your quest for better learning conditions. Give your classroom some class.

76 Helium Can Provide a Cheap Lift

Use helium-filled balloons. It could be the lift you are looking for. Helium can be obtained through any welder's supply or balloon gift shop. Check your yellow pages. Fill the balloons to decorate or to launch (see idea #82). Fill odd-shaped balloons to hand out at the registration table. Helium is not toxic nor very expensive. For this kind of lift, helium is a real bargain.

 ## Balloon Arch Idea #1

Take two pieces of one-half-inch (PVC) plastic water pipe. Connect them together using a half-inch connector. Anchor each end in a concrete block. Next inflate your balloons and tie the two ends together. By twisting these around the plastic pipe you will have an arch that even St. Louis would envy. To decorate the concrete blocks, just wrap them in gift paper. This arch is especially good for outdoor use.

 ## Balloon Arch Idea #2

This arch is easier to put together. You will need helium to fill the balloons. Tie a piece of fishing line to them, just the way you see them at the stores. Now, measure out enough string to double the width of the desired arch. Simply tie the helium filled balloons to the double length of line. The helium will give the arch the needed lift. Adjust the length of the lines to give this arch the look you are seeking. This arch is very good for indoor use. Drafts and air conditioners will cause this style arch to sway. If this is a problem, use idea # 77.

Columns Show Your Pride

Build a set of Roman columns that will set off any stage. You will need the cardboard roll on which carpet comes, 2" x 8" pieces of wood, a little glue, some nails and some paint. The columns act as decorations or podiums for trophies, and they attract attention no matter where they stand. Directions: First, cut two 8" x 8" x 2" blocks of wood. Then, cut two 6" x 6" x 2" blocks of wood. Next, cut the cardboard tube to the desired size. Remember to add 6" to the desired height and then cut. Next, trace the circumference of the tubes onto the blocks of wood and remove the centers. When stacked upon one another this will give the tube extra support. Now stack the 6" squares on the 8" squares and insert the cardboard tube. Secure the tube and the bases with nails and glue. Finally, paint and decorate.

 Add a Service Project Contest to Your VBS

VBS is a great place to teach service to others. Collecting canned goods, clothes, mittens, coats, items for children and retirement homes is a super way to add to the benefits of your program. A contest between the boys and the girls can add to the excitement and the results of your endeavor.

6

ATTENTION-GETTERS

IT BEATS A WHISTLE

81 Try an Attention-Getter

Do you have the problem of waiting five or ten minutes to start your program just to allow people to arrive? Solve this problem by having a special event a half hour before your regular starting time. Try to arrange for the local fire department show off their trucks in the church parking lot. A balloon launch (idea #82), or even a hot air balloon lift-off would attract your neighbors' attention. It also gets your regulars there on time. Outdoor events are the best and it's free publicity. However, indoor events work well, too. Simply arrange your event a half hour before you desire to start your regular program. Publicize the starting time and allow the attention-getter to draw the crowd. After the event, begin the simple process of moving the crowd to your regularly scheduled program. This form of attention-getting is fun and exciting. It also allows you to start on time.

 Balloon Launches Raises Hopes

Nothing is prettier than a rainbow of balloons floating toward the sky. Use 9" round balloons; actually, the bigger the better! Obtain your helium from a balloon bouquet store or a welding supply house. After you've inflated the balloon, use a light weight paper to make name and address tags. That way when the balloon is found it can be returned and the distance can be recorded. Use short strings to attach the name tags to the balloons. Remember, weight is the enemy in a balloon launch. Don't forget to give a prize to the child who's balloon is reported to have traveled the farthest distance by the end of the week.

 Balloon Launch Idea #2

Use the same procedure as before, only in this balloon launch add a spiritual flavor. You could illustrate sound Biblical principles such as hope, prayers rising to God, the rainbow of Noah, beauty, or love. To make this a memorable event have a short devotional and a prayer just before the release of the balloons.

 Balloon Stomps Are a Blast

Put balloons and kids in a room together. Clear the room of any breakables and add a 10 to 1 ratio of

balloons to participants. Next, let the kids go! Allow several minutes for the kids to burst the balloons with their feet. Though loud, it makes for a great time, super pictures, and lots of smiles.

Water Slides Are Good Clean Fun

You need: 4 bails of straw; 1 sheet of 100'x4' plastic (size can be altered to desired length of slide); 1 large bottle of dish soap; 1 water hose; a water supply. Check the sliding area for rocks, sticks, and other dangerous objects and remove them before you start. Scatter the straw out over your designated sliding area. This will act as padding and also help prevent injury from objects you may have missed. Put the plastic "slide way" down over the straw. Soap and wet the plastic, then allow the kids to slide the time away. A running start helps and the slide will work better the more it is used. Don't be discouraged if the first dozen attempts are not spectacular. It will improve. Remember, as always, safety first.

The "Olympic Crowd Raises the Paper Over Its Head to Form a Picture" Picture

You have a crowd. Why not get them all involved? Place poster boards under their chairs so that when they hold it over their heads, it forms a picture. You can use the VBS logo for that year, a picture of Jesus, or whatever fits the theme of the VBS. Draw a grid on the picture. For each square the grid forms on the original picture have a sheet of poster board three or four times larger with the same proportions. Draw the contents of each square grid on a piece of poster board. Paint the poster boards. Have people hold the posterboards over their heads. Photograph or videotape it from a balcony or from the roof of the church–the higher the better. It's a lot of fun and the pictures are great to display.

 ## Light an Eternal Flame

Use the burner out of an old gas grill and you can safely develop an eternal flame. The concept of being a "light to the world" is at the heart of every VBS, so display it proudly. Again, whenever you use fire, please use adult supervision and remember: safety first. Extinguish the flame when it is left unsupervised.

 ## Indoor Torch

If you like the idea of a torch to light the days of your VBS, but there is no way you can do anything like that outdoors, here's an alternative: move the torch indoors. Make your torch by using a household fan and crepe paper streamers. Tape red, yellow, and orange streamers to the grid of your fan. Place the fan, crepe paper side facing the ceiling on two cement blocks. Place a cardboard base to hide the entire apparatus. To light your torch, all you have to do is turn on your fan. Experiment with the speeds on your fan to find the desired effect. From a short distance the crepe paper will dance like a roaring fire, and your Olympic torch will flicker to everyone's delight.

 ## A Fair Is Better Than Average

A fair can be used as a kick-off or as a crowning event to a super week. Your carnival doesn't have to be large, but it can be effective. Dream big and go for it! Use it as an incentive. Give out tickets for registration, for bringing visitors, doing memory work, daily attendance, and bringing your Bible. Set up the games and the food on a ticket only basis. You will create a lot of enthusiasm.

7

MISSIONS

TAPE MEASURING
OUR SUPPORT

90 Make Missions Time a Special Time

Mission support measures your church's faithfulness. Many times we keep missions in mind only as long as they are in sight. When that happens we have let our students and our missionary come up short. Make mission's time a special time. It should last longer than five or ten minutes in the opening or the closing. The kids have to see that missions is a goal worth measuring up to.

 ## Give More Than Your Money

Missions time allows your students to give of themselves to others. Use it as an opportunity to give more than cash. You can encourage the people who attend VBS to write letters or make phone calls to your mission. They can gather things to send. If the mission is local, you can take a field trip. Anyway you look at it, your missionary time is more than a time to give your money—it is a time to give your heart.

 ## Missionaries Like Floods

It is true. Missionaries like floods—floods of mail that is. When missionaries are excited about what they are doing, then other people get excited about what they are doing, too. This could be the chance to let your VBS attenders rain down a flood of mail blessings on some very dedicated people.

 ## Not All Missionaries Eat Bugs

If your missionary is from a foreign land, then take a night and prepare some of their traditional foods. It can be a reminder of "home" to your missionary and it will be a great experience to the kids. The samples you give out don't have to be large, so quantity is not the issue. The kids will get a taste of the mission field.

 ## 94 You Have to Dress the Part

If your missionary comes from a place where the dress is different than to what you are accustomed, then one night dress like they would. Allow the students a day or two to learn about the mission's culture before they gather their costumes. When it comes time to "dress the part," it will be like you've paid your missionary a visit and they will feel at home.

 ## 95 Missionary Surprise

Missionaries are busy and sometimes they don't get to go to their home church. In these cases bring their home church to them. Call their church and have them locate people who know your missionary, and have them write a letter telling stories about your guest. Take time during the week to put together a scrap book. You could even add notes of encouragement. The missionary will never forget this gift. Everyone loves surprises!

 ## 96 Looking for a Missionary? Check Your Missions Committee

When it comes to the question of who to select as your VBS missionary, check with your missions committee. Whether your church supports only one or many missions, this is an excellent time to learn about one of them. You probably would only want to choose one since the time is limited. This could involve your missions committee in VBS.

 Let the Kids Show and Tell

What if your missionary cannot make it in person and all you get is a packet of information? What do you do? Let the kids show and tell. Get a few of your teens to study the information and let them present the mission portion of the VBS program each day. This gives the teens an opportunity to practice teaching roles and to perhaps develop an interest in missions themselves.

 Keep It Up

Who says that you can't emphasize a mission after VBS is over? Why not work a mission time into all of your youth programming all year long. The students could write or call the missionary throughout the year. The extra prayers and encouragement can be great for the missionary and the learning experience is excellent for the kids. Let your students know that missions are important. Start your support and keep it up.

8

REFRESHMENTS

IT'S BREAK TIME!

99 Let's Examine Refreshments

Kids and food–they go together like peanut butter and jelly. So, at VBS, why not make refreshment time special. The traditional cookies and punch may not have the same "punch" they use to have. Be creative! Creative doesn't have to mean more expensive. Popcorn, brownies, fruit, candied apples, snow cones, cheese, crackers, and fruit juices are just a few ways to make refreshment time more appealing.

Snow Cones Are Cool

Snow cones are a traditional favorite and you don't have to have a big machine to make them. Simply buy the flavor syrup and bags of chipped ice. Put ice in paper cups and let the kids choose their favorite flavors. It's a great way to chill out at a totally hot VBS.

 ## Popcorn With a Twist

Make your popcorn in the traditional way, but sprinkle seasoned salt on it. The taste changes completely. It's fast, easy, and even ecologically sound.

 ## Peanut Butter and Honey

Peanut butter is OK by itself, but if you add honey you'll have the whole place a-buzzing. Simply mix the two together and then see how many different things you can find to spread it on: bread, saltines, graham crackers, celery, apples, bananas, potato chips—they're all great!

 ## Honey, I Shrunk the Fruitcicles

Take any cup of fruit, a cup of fruit juice, and a cup of water and blend them together. Pour the concoction into ice cube trays. Add a toothpick and freeze. These miniature fruitcicles are healthy and they taste great!

104 Milk Shake, Rattle, and Whoa!

Find your favorite ice cream, add a special topping, and blend. The results are enough to excite any crowd. You might need to experiment a bit with the recipe, but you will have plenty of volunteers to be your official taster.

 ## 105 Caramel Apples

This treat is one that will make a real sweet impression on your students. It will take some time, but the look on the faces of your students will be more than enough to keep the doctor away.

 ## 106 Yogurt on a Stick

Yogurt has been given a whole new reputation and a whole new taste. Why not put some fruit-flavored yogurt into ice cube trays and freeze it? Stretch plastic over the top of the tray and put in toothpicks. After you freeze the yogurt, you'll have a healthy treat and a lot of happy people.

 ## 107 Climb Every Mountain

For climbing this mountain all you need are some spoons. Make an ice cream mountain. You will need a big bowl or tub and plenty of ice cream. Open the cartons and dump the ice cream into the bowl or tub.

Keep piling on the ice cream until you run out of it. Dish it out or just give them a spoon and let them dig in.

108   Dried Fruit Is a Juicy Treat

Dried fruit—like dried banana chips or apple chips— is a great snack. It doesn't even mess up the carpet when it's spilled. You can buy bags of it wholesale.

Hit the Trail

For camping or western-type themes, have a trail mix. Use any combination of the following ingredients: banana chips, miniature marshmallows, pretzels, chocolate chips, carob chips, peanuts, raisins, or popcorn.

 ## Want a Special Snack?
Check With a Restaurant

If you want something really special find a restaurant that is proud of their recipes and ask them to come and sponsor a night. They may do it free for the advertisement. If not for free, they may negotiate a deal that is reasonable. This is not an idea that could be used every night, but it is suitable for special events.

 ## I Like Your Art—It Tastes Good!

Kids love to express themselves. Have the cookie dough ready. Allow the kids to cut out their cookies and decorate them. Then let them go to class. When break time rolls around their art will have been "fired" and ready for consumption.

 ## Personalized Pizza

Everyone can have their own personalized pizza if you use English muffins. Split the muffin and add pizza sauce. Then have each of the students top their creations as they desire. Set the oven to broil for 250 degrees and cook the pizzas for four to five minutes or until the cheese is melted. This kind of refreshment is something that only VBS can deliver.

Noah's Fruity Ark

Slice and dice fruit into odd shapes. Then allow the students to use toothpicks to hold the fruit together and make "animals." They can lay the fruit flat on a paper plate or make them stand on watermelon legs.

Fun Raisin

Every VBS needs a little "Fun Raisin." Take a piece of bread and cover it with peanut butter. Then allow the students to make faces on the surface of the peanut butter using raisins. They can add smiles, eyes, noses, and hair. It's as much fun to make as it is to eat.

A Refreshing Theme

Keep in mind the theme of the VBS when making the menu for snack time. Look at the lesson. Does it have to do with a food or concept that can be applied to your refreshments? How about trail mix for the exodus from Egypt? Call it manna. How about honey for Samson? It could be the connection you've been waiting for.

Check With Your High School

Some high schools have popcorn poppers and cotton candy machines that they may loan. All you can do is ask and all they can say is "yes" or "no." If you borrow, be responsible and clean it up even better then when you received it. They will be so appreciative that they will want you to borrow it after every ball game.

 ## Have a Cake-Baking Contest

Announce that on one of the days of VBS there will be a cake-baking contest. The entries will be judged and prizes given. All entries become the property of the VBS. There is sure to be enough refreshments for everyone. In this contest the kids will be the winners.

CONTESTS

TIME TO INSTALL THE ELECTRICITY

 118 **Add a Jolt to Your VBS**

Electricity makes things happen. A light bulb is nice—too light to be a paper weight, but I still like them. They're best used when the "juice" is added. Things just seem to brighten when the electricity and the bulb works together. Contests are that way too. You can still do a lot of things without them, but they work with your VBS to brighten up the surroundings. Use them wisely and a contest can electrify your entire VBS.

 ## Contests Raise Attendance

Attendance contests really do add excitement to VBS. Even though the controversy still rages whether or not competition is good for the soul, a contest can do great things when kept in proper perspective. Remember, VBS has a higher purpose than staging a contest. Make sure that the VBS runs the contest and that the contest doesn't run the VBS.

 ## Boys Versus Girls: A Natural Contest

The battle between the sexes is as old as history itself. Don't fight it. Use it! Whether it is attendance, offering, Bible memorization, or any other desired task, challenge the two groups to playfully compete and excitement will build. It's a natural.

 ## Pies Add Excitement

I don't know who was the first guy to ever throw a pie into someone else's face, but I'd like to shake his hand. He gave to us one of the best smile-makers ever invented. Use them when you hit a contest goal. Use them when you want to have fun. Use them on an authority figure. Just use them! Always use common sense when throwing pies. Cover the person with plastic for easy clean up. Ask the recipient's permission before you throw. Pre-stage each event for the best possible results. Use whipped cream instead of shaving cream — it is easier on the eyes.

 Make an Offering Scale

Offering can be a fun time during VBS. By the use of an offering scale you will be able to weigh the

difference. Build a large scale, and have your offering placed in the trays. You might want to convert paper money into coins. The side with the heaviest offering wins for the day. No matter how you divide the teams, the excitement of the competition will help everyone catch VBS fever.

 Shout It Out

VBS is a high energy time. Why not let the kids shout it out in the form of a contest? Divide the groups into sections and let them, one section at at time, see who can shout the loudest. They can shout a part of a memory verse or a nonsense phrase. The purpose is simply fun and excitement. I've never met a kid yet who didn't love it when their parents said, "I heard you all the way out here!" Besides, VBS is worth shouting about.

 Let 'em "Sock" It Out

Anytime the missions have a need for clothing, socks are listed among the needs. With slogans like, "Sock Your Missionary" or "VBS Will Knock Your Socks Off!" you can have a great time meeting a need. When the students bring their new clean socks, they can hang them on a branch to create a sock tree, or you could have a "sock box," or you could have the director stand up front and the kids could "sock it to him."

Visualize Your Contest

Any contest works better if there is something to see. Whether it's a colorful board or a projected slide, seeing is believing. If there are movable parts, such as a little boy or girl moving toward a goal, then the students can relate to your goal much better. The bigger and brighter, the better. Help your VBS "see" the goal!

 ## Can Your VBS

In this day of environmental awareness, this is a great time to can your VBS. I'm talking about aluminum cans. Stack them high or lay them around in plastic bags and watch the contest grow. Then at the end of the week cash them in. The cash can be an addition to the missionary offering. It is fun and it could make a ton–if not just a couple of hundred pounds–of difference

 ## Talent Shows Could Help "Rap" Up Your VBS

Whether you consider rap a talent or not, a showing of talents could be a real winner. Allowing your young people and your workers to display their talents could give you a list of resources long enough for the whole year. Let them sing, and play. Let them show their art and read their writings. Let them throw their fast ball in the auditorium, any of these will throw a real curve to boredom.

Externally Speaking, It's Internal That Counts!

Contests are external motivations that open doors. That is the purpose of a good contest: to open doors toward excellence. Anything can become a contest: scripture memorization, attendance, bringing your Bible. The real pay-off is when the students walk through the "doors" after the contest is over. They have experienced Bible study and they continue to do it on their own. They have enjoyed helping others and they make it a lifestyle. They have internalized it. So speaking from the outside, it's the inside that counts.

10

RECREATION

WHERE GOOFING AROUND
ON THE JOB IS OK

129 **No Pressure**

When it comes to recreation, there should be no
pressure at all. Stay cool. This is a time when you can
get to know your students. If you are calm, cool, and
collected, they will be, too.

70

Recreation on Purpose

Have you ever stopped to think why VBS includes a recreation time? First, it allows the kids to move. Your students may look like small adults, but they aren't. They have a power generator that just won't quit. Recreation is a time when they can drain-off some of that extra energy.

 Build Relationships During Recreation

The second reason that recreation is important to VBS programs is the relationships that can be built. Change your mind-set when it comes to choosing the recreation staff. Find people that are interested in making friends. Watch out for the "jocks" that want to play and win. If possible, over-staff the recreation team so that there will be more relationship opportunities. You'll make some friends. What better way is there to win?

 Variations on Volleyball #1: Play It Indoors

It's raining and you can't go out? No problem. Just play volleyball indoors. Let me explain before you panic or make an enemy out of the church janitor. You don't use a normal volleyball—you use a balloon. The set-up is simple. Set a row of chairs down the middle of the room. This acts as your net. Then have the two teams sit on the floor. The rest of the rules are followed as usual. It's fun, safe, and it doesn't hurt when the ball hits you in the head.

 ## Variations on Volleyball #2: Switch the Ball

The neat thing about volleyball is that by switching the ball, you've created a whole new game. You can use water balloons, an inexpensive play ball, or a weather balloon (best for indoor/gymnasium use). Change the size or the weight of the ball and you've created a monstrously fun time.

 ## Variations on Volleyball #3: First You Add Water, Then You Add Air

Find a punch ball balloon and add about two cups of water. Then inflate to desired size and tie the top. The balloon is tough enough to take a pounding and different enough that you will never know where it is going to come down. You've created a volleyball that will keep everyone guessing. Keep a couple of extra punch ball balloons on hand, because even the toughest balloons are no match for a group of kids having fun.

 ## Variations on Volleyball #4: Water Balloon Volleyball

You'll need two old bed sheets and a bucket full of water balloons. Give a sheet to each team. Instruct the teams to have each player grab the ends of their sheet. Place a water balloon in the center of one of the team's sheet. That team's members cooperate and use the sheet to propel the water balloon over the net. The other team tries to catch it. If the other team catches the balloon without it bursting, they get a point. The other team then propels the water balloon back to the first team and so on. The secret is for the team with the balloon to crowd together then take a step back and lift the sheet over their heads to send the balloon flying. The results are hilarious. Oh, make sure that the person who donates the sheets doesn't expect to see them again because they might get torn.

No-Foul Baseball in the Round

Here are some twists to one of America's favorite pastimes. Change the rules to baseball. In No-Foul Baseball both teams have the same pitcher. The players run the bases backward. There are no foul balls. Every ball that is hit is considered fair. The fielding team will need to have fielders in front of and behind home plate. Everyone must bat opposite-handed. With these simple changes you have "baseball in the round." It's fun breaking tradition. It's also fun to watch the kids take off toward traditional first base and then remember that they are suppose to run the bases backward. Play ball!

 Don't Plan

"Don't plan a recreation period!" Have all the equipment ready and allow the kids to decide what they want to play. They can organize a kickball game or a game of tag. This allows them to develop some interpersonal skills and they won't even realize that they're learning.

 Watch for the Loner

The fact is that not everyone is athletic and that is OK. Be on the watch for the student that shows no interest in the activities of the moment. Encourage them to be active, but don't force them. The concept is to make a friend, not a gold-medal winner.

 139 **My Grandparents Know How to Play**

To look at them today, you could never imagine that they used to play games. They are sophisticated and proper, but to hear the stories about the games they used to play when they were kids—Wow! Today's kids are really complicated, and they could use an injection of simple games from the "good 'ole days." Find a grandparent or two and ask them what games they played when they were young. You'll get more ideas than you know what to do with and you may even get a couple of great recreation directors.

11

FOLLOW UP

OPENING THE DOORS

140 Make Your Closing Count

Your closing is the best time for you to introduce your church to the community. Excitement and anticipation fill the air. Keep your closing high-powered and relatively short. A long closing will discourage visitors from returning visit any time soon.

Your Closing Is Your Best Invitation to Next Year's VBS

The week has been tremendous, so make sure your closing reflects that to your parents. They need to hear about the highlights of the week. Make them want to experience the excitement that you've generated. If your closing is good, then you've opened the doors of your church to your visitors and thrown out a welcome mat for all to see. Your closing can be a great invitation for everyone to come back again.

 A Short Closing Will Drive the Excitement Home

Closing programs are important, but stop and think. It has been a great week–don't sell it to the parents any differently. Design your closing program to be no longer than an hour and fifteen minutes. Don't fill it with "war stories", like, "Little Joey said this . . . " or, "Mrs. Jones' class did that . . . ." Pack your closing full of excitement and color. This will allow the parents to experience the fun instead of just learning about it. It will also let them see the quality of your care.

 Have a Teacher and Volunteer Recognition

Your workers are your most valuable resource. They have worked like troopers, so let them know you appreciate it. A banquet or an award ceremony is just the thing. Everybody likes a pat on the back, so don't forget to recognize your workers.

Group Pictures Show Your Class

People are vain, so use it to generate VBS excitement. Announce that group pictures will be taken early in the week. Watch the people show up on time just to

be in the picture. Make copies for the record, then sell the rest to the VBS crowd at cost. You could even present them as awards at the end of the week. It shows that an individual "graduated" from a week of

Vacation Bible School. These pictures are not a yearbook, but they do show you have class.

 ## 145 Use Slides to Recap the Week

Know somebody who has a 35mm camera? Great! Then you have a great way to recap your VBS. Call your local film development stores to check prices and development time. It can be done in as little as four hours at some stores. Take pictures of smiles, activities, and classes. Add a little theme music and you're set. Your VBS ought to be in pictures.

 ## 146 Use Video to Recap the Week

Camcorders are everywhere. Why not go high-tech with your closing? Videotape different activities throughout the week and have a "news cast" type of closing. Your two anchor people can do interviews and recaps to a successful week!

 ## 147 Follow-Up Idea #1: The Teacher's Note

Follow-up on visitors is vital in any successful VBS and it can be done by the numbers. A teacher's note is important. The student has spent the week with this person and a bond has developed. Have the teacher write a note or postcard to each of their students the week following VBS. The sooner this is done, the better. The students will feel welcomed again!

Follow-Up Idea #2:
The Teacher's Phone Call

Some kids get lots of phone calls, but rarely is it good news if it's an adult on the other end. Break the trend. Have your teachers call their students after VBS is over and invite them to become active in the church.

Follow-Up Idea #3:
Youth Mailing List

Put the name of everyone who attended your VBS on a youth mailing list. Then mail information to them about the youth programs at your church. Using computer or copier labels will save time. This will get the word out that you really care about youth.

Follow-Up Idea #4:
Letter

Another form of follow-up is the U.S. Mail. A letter from the church will impress kids. They treasure what little mail they get. It'll hang on the walls of their rooms, on the refrigerators, and will stay in their "treasure boxes" for weeks! Wow! It's like a free billboard right in the kid's room.

Follow-Up Idea #5:
The Sunday School

In the Sunday School, you've got a whole battalion of follow-up specialists. A contact from the Sunday school teacher would allow a natural transition from VBS, a once-a-year program, to Sunday school, a weekly program.

Copy Registration Information for Your Sunday School

VBS registration has been great. Now that you have all these cards, what do you do with them? Why not photocopy the entire card and pass out the information to the corresponding Sunday school teacher and youth group sponsor! The copies save time and effort, and they contain all the information that is needed for a great follow-up program.

"Thank You" Notes Are the First Step of Next Year's VBS

"Always remember to say please and thank you." It was true then and it's true with your volunteers now. They've worked hard and a steak dinner would be great, but a nice "thank you" note is an effective alternative. People like to know they've been appreciated and volunteers are not different. By the way, this will help in your recruitment of volunteers next year. Don't forget to write "Thanks!"

12

CLOSING THOUGHTS

SWEEPING THE SAWDUST

154 Don't Get Discouraged

It's simple to say, but tough to do. Rome wasn't built in a day, nor was any VBS program (at least not one worth doing!). It takes months and even years to develop the type of program you desire. Keep on working and praying toward the goals you've set. The Lord will bless.

155 Have a Positive Attitude

Your attitude will reflect in your workers. You smile and they will smile. If you frown and grump, then they will frown and grump. Make sure your attitude is positive at all times. Even crisis situations can be handled with a positive attitude. Your attitude will make a difference.

APPENDIX A

It sounds like a lot of paper work, but charts like these make it easier. The benefits you reap from keeping records far outweigh the hassles. Keep statistics on everything. Here are sample charts to put statistics in perspective. You may use the charts on these pages and invent any other record charts you may need for your particular church.

REGISTRATION

Age Group	Last Year	This Year	Amount of Material	Rm. #
Nursery				
2 year olds				
3 year olds				
4 year olds				
Kindergarten				
First Grade				
Second Grade				
Third Grade				
Fourth Grade				
Fifth Grade				
Sixth Grade				
Seventh Grade				
Eighth Grade				
Senior High				
Adult				

TOTAL DAILY ATTENDANCE

Day	Date	Total Attendance	Weather	Last Year's Attendance
1				
2				
3				
4				
5				
6				
7				
8				
9				
10				

COSTS

Item	This Year	Last Year
Materials		
Publicity		
Refreshments		
Crafts		
Recreation		
Special Events		
Special Speakers		

AVERAGE ATTENDANCE

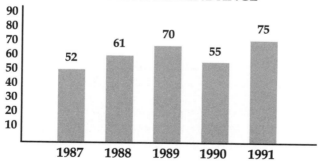

APPENDIX B

See Idea #9: Use a Directing Committee

AN EXAMPLE OF A VBS DIRECTING COMMITTEE

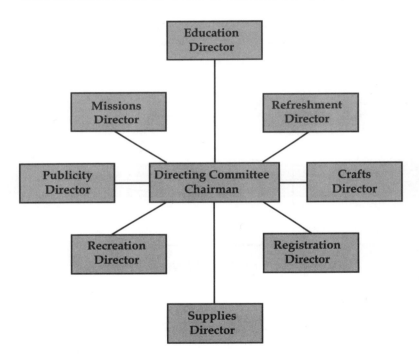

Try using a VBS Directing Committee. The Director of VBS serves as chairman and sees that every aspect of VBS is directed by a competent person. VBS will run smoother when everyone does his or her part.

APPENDIX C

See Idea #11: Write Job Descriptions

The director of VBS should give job descriptions to every person who volunteers their time and abilities to VBS. Here is an example of a job description for a VBS Patrol Person:

VBS PATROL PERSON

Here are your responsibilities:
1. Be at the church between 6:00p.m. and 6:15p.m. Help parents as they drop off their children in the parking lot.
2. Keep the parking lot safe for people.
3. Slow cars that are moving too fast.
4. Record the name of visiting children who are dropped off by car and the license plate number of the car that dropped them off.
5. Keep children from playing in the parking lot.
6. During VBS, roam the halls in search of lost persons.
7. Offer a helping hand to anyone who needs it.
8. Move furniture or props if needed.
9. Each day after VBS, direct parking lot traffic.
10. Stay until last child has been picked up by the person who dropped them off at the church.
11. Most importantly, greet people with a smile and a handshake when they arrive at VBS.

Using this format, write job descriptions for each director, each teacher, each assistant teacher, and every person helping with the VBS.

APPENDIX D

See Idea #'s 14, 15: Prayer Warriors

You might want to send a letter like the one below to those whom have been selected specifically to pray for VBS:

Dear Prayer Warrior,

Thank you so much for volunteering your time to pray for our Vacation Bible School. VBS is such an effective ministry in teaching people about the love of our Lord. Please take time every day, from now until the end of VBS to pray for the following:

1. That the love of God will reach those who attend our VBS.
2. That things will run as smoothly as possible.
3. That God will turn obstacles into opportunities.
4. For all our teachers.
5. For all our assistant teachers.
6. For all of our craft teachers.
7. For our missionary and his mission.
8. For our refreshment committee, recreation committee, teen helpers, music leader and other VBS workers.
9. That we will make first-time visitors feel welcomed.
10. That the people, both children and adult, will learn about the love of Jesus.

> Sincerely yours,
> John Cutshall
> VBS Director

If you compile a list with more items than those listed above, you could divide the items into several separate lists and give each list to a different group of people.

APPENDIX E

See Idea #26: Develop an Evaluation Form and Use It

At the end of VBS pass out an evaluation form similar to the one below to the teachers and VBS workers.

VBS EVALUATION FORM

This year's VBS was an experience that we all can remember for a long time. The excitement, the songs, the spreading of God's Word, it was a valid effort to bring glory to God! I would appreciate your taking a few moments to fill out this evaluation. Thank you in advance for your time in this effort and thank you even more for this past week.

—John

Personal Information
1. How many years have you worked in VBS?
2. What age group did you work with this year?

Structure of VBS
1. What was the teacher/student ratio in your class?
2. Did you have enough time in each of your nightly areas? Place an "X" under the appropriate title for each area.

	AREA		
	Not Enough	Enough	Too Much
Lesson			
Crafts			
Refreshments			
Recreation			
Opening			
Missions Time			
Closing			

3. Was our missionary time effective? __ Yes __ No

Areas of VBS Evaluation

Check the box below the appropriate number. 1 means very poor, 5
means average, and 10 means very good.

AREA

	1	2	3	4	5	6	7	8	9	10
Publicity										
Registration										
Refreshments										
Patrol										
Recreation										
Transportation										
Nursery										
2's & 3's										
4's & 5's										
Grades 1 & 2										
Grades 3 & 4										
Grades 5 & 6										
Grades 7 & 8										
Grades 9-12										
Adults										
Opening										
VBS in General										

You may use the back of this page for any additional comments
concerning the rating you have given any particular category.

APPENDIX F

See Idea #s 46-49: Newspaper Advertisement

You could create ads similar to the following and buy a space in your local city or neighborhood newspaper. This one is aimed toward parents:

ARE THE KIDS DRIVING YOU CRAZY?

Wouldn't you love a break before school starts? Do a little shopping without trailing the whole crew?

Well now's your chance! At First Church we care about your family! We even have a full time minister that handles our youth programs!

We care.

You may have seen other youth programs but nobody does them like us!

Bring your kids to a week of Bible School Events! They'll love it and you'll get a break!

August 14-19

6:30 p.m. to 9:00 p.m.

For more information call 555-9061.

First Church 1744 Main Street

This one aims for teenagers:

DON'T BE LEFT OUT!

You know how we all hang out at the mall just to see each other? And you know how everyone's always trying to run us off? Well, I've got the perfect place to meet. Your Mom won't mind you going. They want us to come! It's the First Church! Now don't be thinkin' this is gonna be lame. They know what we like to do! They're gonna have:

A LIVE BAND!

FRIENDS!

FOOD TO SCARF!

VIDEOS!

AWESOME GAMES!

A JAMMIN' GOOD TIME!

So call your friends! Don't come alone! It's a great chance to get together before school starts and it's gonna be a blast!

August 14-19   **6:00 p.m. to 9:00 p.m.**

First Church
1744 Main Street

INDEX

About the Author

John Cutshall has two basic beliefs when it comes to fixing anything. The first is, "If it needs repaired, beat it with a hammer." His second belief is similar: "If a hammer won't fix it, then it is beyond repair and you need to buy a new one."

Fortunately he does not apply these beliefs to Vacation Bible Schools. John has twelve years of youth ministry experience. Through those years he challenged himself to create a VBS that energizes the church and the surrounding community.

He is the Director of Communications and an Instructor of Youth Ministries at Cincinnati Bible College & Seminary where he received his Bachelor of Arts in Christian Education and his Master of Arts in Practical Ministries. He is President of Quality Youth Productions, Inc., a consultation company that helps churches minister to youth.